Write the Story of You

The Book Only YOU Can Write

Jim McCarthy

— Expanded Edition —

JMcontent, LLC

Paperback ISBN: 979-8-9901356-0-4

Amazon Paperback ISBN:

Ebook ISBN: 979-8-9901356-1-1

Contents

Foreword

I wish, about 40 years ago, someone would have pointed out to me that one day I could no longer learn more about so many people I admired. I'm embarrassed to count the number of those who have influenced my life, or even crossed my path, about whom I learned so little. They were colleagues, acquaintances, relatives, and loved ones, and many have taken their stories with them when they died.

I'm hoping you won't do the same.

If you feel you haven't enough life experience to write an autobiography, you're in the right place. We only talk about writing your memoirs here, and you can start a memoir at any age. We'll show you how you can do that.

Editor's Note

The following pages contain the complete original text of Write the Story of You, along with three new chapters that expand on the original material. The new chapters—"The Power of Sensory Detail," "Handling the Hard Stuff," and "Telling Your Story Out Loud: The Recorded Memoir"—appear at the end of the book and are designed to be read after the original seven secrets. They carry forward the same spirit we tried to establish from the first page, and the hope that you are convinced that your story is worth telling.

Introduction

Hello, I'm Jim McCarthy, and I'm here to encourage you to think about becoming a storyteller, because you have a story to tell that no one else can.

No doubt many people on earth share your name. Some may even look like you and even share some of your personality traits.

But not one person has lived your life: experienced your joys, your sorrows, your achievements, your opportunities, your successes, and your failures. That makes you the unique individual you are today, and it is why you need to draft the story.

What inspired me to write this book is a memoir I once edited. It was written by a lady whose name in childhood was **"Patsy Edelbrock,"** and she lived one of the most remarkable lives of anyone I've ever known. Seeing her finished manuscript caused me to reflect on many others I've known who never considered doing the same. The details of their lives are lost forever, and I hope yours won't meet the same fate.

I'd like to help you with a straightforward set of suggestions to get you started and to nurture your motivation to see the project through to whatever end you want to take it.

I retired from about forty years in the travel business, spending more than half that time as a corporate trainer, and much of the rest as a retail travel agent. I have authored articles and newsletters, lesson plans and manuals, and I have taught adults to do a lot of things they thought they never could, all over the USA and in Europe.

So, please don't shy away from this challenge because you think you must be an author first, or an English major, or a grammarian. None of that matters if that's what is keeping you from getting started.

Patsy's memoir was about 40,000 words—almost 150 pages in print, but she started it as I would encourage you to begin yours—by jotting down your recollection of a single day's events. Your journey begins with a pencil and paper, and three or four brief paragraphs.

In this book, I think you'll find many tips and tricks you need to keep you going. I hope you'll find encouragement from others following some of the book's ideas, as they work on their projects like you're working on yours. I will share resources I have used when I think they will help, and you might even connect with others whose progress is on pace with yours.

We all share at least one common interest, individually and collectively, to write the Story of "You."

The Beginner's Guide to Writing Your Memoir

This book was inspired by missed opportunities. My life has been blessed by associations with several remarkable people, most of whom have passed on to their just rewards—leaving behind no record of the details of their lives. None was a "Celebrity," none was "Famous." Most were as common as your next-door neighbor, but all of them experienced unique moments in their lives, specifics of which are now lost forever:

A pre-teen Dutch boy in Indonesia who spent WWII in a Japanese POW camp then became an officer in the Dutch Merchant Marine. He emigrated to the US, married, and joined Hughes Aircraft as an aeronautical engineer, and died at age 56 (complications of his traumatic youth?) . . .

Son of a farmer and daughter of a lighthouse keeper married for 70 years; started their family in the mid-depression, then raised six sons on the single income of a blue-collar civil servant.

The one I will reference most often throughout these pages is one of my favorite successes. I'll call her **"Patsy,"** and she may be the most remarkable of them all. Patsy was the inspiration for an earlier blog, which has become this book. The process she used to produce her 150-page memoir is the one I've recommended to all of you because it is uncomplicated, easily managed, and very productive.

I was pleased with the results once I edited her manuscript, then proofread it and had it published. What astounded me was to see the therapeutic effect it had on the author herself, as she re-read it several times after its publication. In her 80s, Patsy found closure with the unpleasant moments of her childhood. It was a worthy reward to a non-writer, who got started by jotting down a few notes.

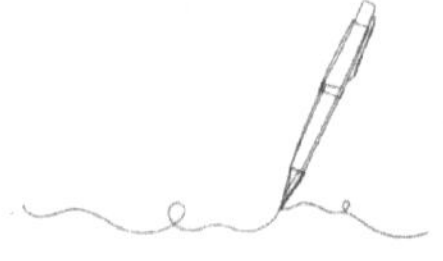

WHAT IS A MEMOIR?

Your memoirs will be a collection of individual moments from your past life. These are written records of anything you experienced: a single moment or event, or a period of any length—your first day at school, your college years, your honeymoon, or your daughter's first Christmas.

The terms "Memoir" and "Memoirs" are often considered synonymous but, technically, the latter term is a collection of the former. The cover of Patsy's book reads, *"Snakes on the Porch, A Memoir."* Since each of its 20 chapters is a separate memoir, the cover might more correctly read "Memoirs."

One Way to Get Started with Your Memoir

All you need to begin is a recollection, a pencil and paper, and a place to jot one down on the other. The thoughts you record today need not connect with anything you wrote yesterday or be in any order; there will be time to do that later, in your "editing" phase.

A later part of the book will address that process, give you suggestions on the easiest way to do it, and add a few tips on what not to do.

Tips for Success in Writing a Memoir

You can begin writing your memories as they occur to you. Don't feel you need to embellish each one before you move on to the next. If you start with a stack of 3x5 cards, you could just jot down a thought you want to develop later on each of them.

That will give you a good outline when the time comes to move your notes onto the written page. Patsy did this on-and-off for almost two years. After that, the editing, proofreading, formatting, and publication took only a few short months of free time.

To digress briefly, another method some use before starting with the 3x5 card notes is to "chart" the entire range of years you're covering. I've done this starting with a large piece of paper, like the clear back of a desk calendar (usually about 16x22 inches). Measure and mark two inches along each edge, then connect the dots to form 2-inch squares over the whole page. You should get 80-90 two-inch squares, each representing a year, noted in the corner of each square. As you think of an event, write a word or two to note it in the year's square where it happened. This will help you both in filling out more 3x5 cards and when you organize them later.

COMMON QUESTIONS/FAQ ABOUT WRITING A MEMOIR

How is a memoir different from an autobiography? An autobiography would be a chronological record of your life, at least from birth to the present, whereas memoirs are usually recorded in any order, and entire portions can be left out altogether. Individual events may focus mostly on the more pleasant or successful memories while ignoring any darker moments. This book focuses only on memoirs.

Do I need to be a writer? If you paid enough attention in the first grade to know how to put words on paper, you have the same skill with which any writer, past or present, has started. Even if you cannot do that (disabled? infirm?) recording your story is still important, and you can discuss the content of your work with someone who can write it down for you. **"Content"** is a writer's term to describe the text of a manuscript, blog, letter, etc.

What tools do I need? Anything that records your thoughts. The first memoirs were written on animal hides and stone tablets, but laptop computers have pretty well destroyed the marble-and-chisel markets, and they're a lot quieter. "Big Chief" yellow tablets and 3x5 cards are cheaper and more portable.

Can I make money with my story? Not likely, unless you're famous for having found a cure for dandruff, or for mapping the coastline of Antarctica from your kayak. You could convert your memoirs into an action novel to make money, but then it would be more like many autobiographies, and we're only covering memoirs here.

What is the cost? Anywhere from $1.25 for a pencil and paper up to your whole allowance, depending on what you plan to do with the finished product. In the earliest pages of this series, we'll start with your first thoughts about what you want to do with the finished product. Some may plan to publish an eBook (almost free), a paperback (a little more expensive), or nothing at all. Any option is good if it reflects your goals and objectives.

How old should I be before I begin? How old should I be before I begin? You are never too young to write a memoir but, if it is yours, it helps to have some life experiences to report.

Seriously, at any age, you know people who have amazing stories to tell and, while they're still in possession of their memories and faculties, what greater compliment than to encourage them to "spill the beans" for you?

THE LAST THING YOU NEED TO KNOW ABOUT GETTING STARTED

Next, we'll be discussing three things you'll use to get started: an Outline, your Research, and Organizing.

- Many of the content topics you collected for your **outline** will become a complete chapter in your memoir; some combine with other topics to complete a chapter.
- Your **research** will have produced more detail, some documentation, and maybe a few photos to dress up the cover, and the finished pages.
- Your o**rganizing** has just begun, but it has put you in a good position to enjoy the most fun part of writing your memoir—**WRITING YOUR MEMOIR!**
- You're in a splendid position to start your "Content" phase, but first, a few important reminders:
- As you put this all together, it may be a good time to look at your goals again. One thing we didn't include in those goals may be the most important one of all—this is an exciting thing you are starting; no matter how you approach it, make it **FUN**. There's no need to feel pressure;

you're under no time constraints. If you feel it is a chore, take a break, and don't come back until you genuinely want to.

- Throughout the entire process, keep envisioning the finished product. You're not just authoring a book; you're finally telling the world the story of YOU!
- Everyone else reading this book is probably feeling the same as you are. If your doubts and fears aren't something you can discuss with a trusted friend or fellow member of a writers' group, try chatting with someone online. The "Resources" pages further back in this book may suggest a good place to start.
- I've always been amazed at the caliber of talented editors and coaches who often show up in online chats, freely sharing opinions and advice for which their clients and students are happy to pay big bucks.
- What else can we do to get you started? Tell us your story.

Ready, set, write!

Let's Get Started:

Maybe you've thought of writing your memoirs before. If so, what has kept you from starting? Or maybe you started already but have put your project on hold. Either way, give some thought to these questions so we can plan for your success, then we'll take steps to help you achieve your goals:

Why are you writing this?

- To honor those in your past?
- To get something "off your chest?"
- To keep it as a family record?
- To publish an eBook? a paperback?
- Anything else . . .

Your answer to this becomes your goal, and it may be the most important step to your success. Your reasons for doing this work may change, even several times, during the "content" phase—that is, the part where you begin by writing the outlines and the text that will eventually become your finished manuscript.

This goal may change somewhat but that is normal because, as you progress, you will recollect things long forgotten and you may even discover other events for the first time, as you research.

Don't new goals mean starting all over?

Not at all. Changing your goals is an encouraging sign that the writing process is getting easier for you. As you proceed, much of your content will almost write itself, as words and ideas seem to "appear" to you in your conversations.

3 Tips to Get You Started: Outline, Research, Organize. . .

Tip 1: Begin Collecting "Content" Topics

- Decide on the most comfortable way/place to record your thoughts as they occur to you. First, plan on momentary "jot down" sessions to get an **outline** started: on 3x5 cards, on a notepad, or if you prefer, a laptop/smartphone. It will help later if each short topic is on a separate piece of paper (or card). You will see why when we talk about the organizing step.

- Keep it simple. Organize nothing yet. Rather, record each thought as it pops into your mind; write it down, then put it aside.
- As you record each note or event, it will help if you can identify it with the approximate date when it occurred or happened (just the year will be fine).

Tip 2: Check your family files for details

- While you continue collecting topics for your outline, begin looking through any family files and albums for personal records, old letters, photos, and anything that will fill in forgotten details.
- If this **research** suggests topics you may have overlooked so far, record each one as a new content topic, including its date (year).
- Continue this research throughout the rest of your project, as it will come in handy when the editing phase begins later.

Tip 3: Organize at your leisure

- Once you are getting comfortable with how your outline and research is developing, you can start thinking about how all this will come together.

You're free to **organize** some of what you've collected, but **ONLY** if it doesn't interfere with what you've been doing so far. Do not stress yourself.

- Start sorting each of your topics according to the date you've recorded on it.
- Sort by year, first, then within any year, by the month, etc.
- Your memoir need not be chronological, but this arrangement will help with your perspective, as you begin the next phase—the "writing-your-content" part.

You don't need a degree or to be an author. You don't even have to be good at grammar and punctuation to get the process started. All you need to do is supply what only you have—the details of your story.

While you are collecting the events that will make up your memoirs someday, you could start learning the process by helping with the memoirs of someone else. It could be a parent, a mentor, another relative or just someone you respect and admire.

There is a unique book inside each of us, but most of those have never been written.

I hope to change that, by inviting you to consider following some ideas in this book, and maybe even to interact with others doing the same.

Glance through these pages until you feel comfortable with what we're doing. We will try to progress in an orderly fashion but will not suggest there is a "best way" to do any of it. Where there are alternative means of doing anything, we'll try to point that out.

Each option will try to give you some direction, answer questions and offer input on some tools you may use. Should you run into difficulties with your project, you'll find comments from others who may describe solutions they used to solve similar problems.

That is an advantage to working with a writers group, or someone also working on his/her memoir, but you will do your best work if you feel no obligation to anyone else or impose any pressure of time on yourself.

Only you should control that, because the best way to succeed in this project is, more than anything else, to keep it something so enjoyable and so much fun that you can't wait to get back to it.

The Writers Block Myth . . .

You may have heard the term "writer's block" tossed around, especially if you've spent time around professional writers. Teachers and coaches might even write books about how to overcome this "plague of the creative mind," but I've learned to follow an easier solution.

I made my living for many years as a ghostwriter in the corporate world of non-fiction, and I don't recall ever suffering from writers block for as much as a minute. My secret? Deny it!

If you don't see, hear, smell, touch, or taste something, as far as your mind knows, it doesn't exist. I've found you can tune out your senses and, as far as your mind cares, it doesn't exist, either. It's your mind, so you control what you recognize as reality and what you do not. Let me give you an illustration:

I spent my corporate years in the travel business, both as

an airline instructor and as a travel agent. In both capacities, many of my customers/clients were often first-timers at either flying or cruising who had to deal with doubts and fears about travel before they could proceed with their plans. Each of them who followed my advice returned from his/her flight or cruise as a seasoned veteran traveler, and every one of them returned to my office for future travel arrangements.

When each of them first came to my office to pick up travel documents, we took time for a simple chat. We agreed it wasn't a good idea to start the departure day with a big meal and, before boarding the plane or the ship, it was best to avoid stimulants of any kind.

Most important, from the moment they left my office that day, airsickness and seasickness didn't exist for them. The words didn't exist, nor did any reality. If spoken in their presence, they couldn't even recognize the sound of those words—until they had completed at least the first day of their travels.

Their efforts were required only for the first day, and after that, the threat disappeared.

I've always found it works the same for writer's block, for those who work at it briefly.

The reason you won't have to worry about writer's block —at least for writing your memoir—is each idea you jot down as you develop your outline is an isolated event, at first. Until you begin to "flesh out" some of those ideas and they form content, then chapters, there's nothing to "block."

7 Secrets for a Quick and Easy Way to

Start Your Memoir

by

Jim McCarthy

There are many ways to write a memoir. I have tried several, but this book will focus on only one. I've found it's one that works well for anyone and seems to make writing easier, especially for the "non-writer." There is nothing magical about this process, and it's so flexible you can adapt it to your lifestyle any way you like. Let's start with #1.

SECRET #1:

Know that you can do this; believing in yourself is vital.

You are the ONLY one who can do this, because who knows more about your life than you? Until you finish this document, what and who you are will remain a secret to the world.

Writing your memoir will change that, and who better than you can write it?

What you write is more important than how it is written. Just write the way you talk and don't worry about the "King's English" for now.

Yes, you could hire professional writers to clean up things like grammar and punctuation. You could even dictate the facts to a ghostwriter—but no one will enjoy reading your story more than when you have written it in your own conversational style.

Once you can believe in what you are doing, the floodgates will open, and the facts will grow. You will look forward to each time you sit down to add more to your work and that, too, will keep you motivated.

Activity:

As you prepare to begin your project, start developing a picture in your mind of what the finished work will look like: A simple manuscript? A published work? A photo on the book's cover? A table of contents with 20 chapters? A list of Illustrations?

Keep that image in mind as you progress all the way to the finish line.

SECRET #2:

Find your "creative space." It should be a spot where you can work comfortably, feel secure and be uninterrupted.

This will become more important in the second phase of your project—where you organize your notes into an outline but, if you can do it from the beginning, all the better. Don't limit yourself to working only when you can get to your creative space, but try to have one ready for those moments when more thoughtful reflection is needed. The more time you can spend in this spot, the more you will enjoy planning and writing, and that is the most important goal.

Not everyone has the luxury of working in a dedicated place but choose the best spot where you can be comfortable, at least. Once you have had productive experiences there a few times, your unconscious mind will recognize it as the place where it is supposed to turn on your "creative juices" so you can get to work doing what you enjoy.

Activity:

If no space comes to mind at first, think of where you have found a favorite space to read or do other relaxing things lately. It may be in your bedroom, or the library downtown. It may be in your backyard or at the beach. Try to think of two or three locations and see what works best for you at each of them.

Secret #3:

You are a writer if you can put words on paper. "I'm not a Writer" is the objection I hear most often, but that is not important.

Most of us will never be authors, but that does not mean you can't put words on paper, and that is all it takes to get you started on your adventure. Just start recording:

- Events recollected as they affected you.
- Lessons you learned from your experiences
- Moments of victory over the obstacles you encountered

- Days of hardship or sadness, and how you handled them.

Any or all of the above are what you need to get started. Nothing says you must include all those topics—some you may wish to exclude, and that's O.K. That's the beauty of a memoir; you can record as much as you want, and avoid all the rest of it, if that's your choice.

You can put it down on paper in any order you like. YOU decide everything that's in your manuscript, and the order in which it appears, as well.

An autobiography starts at the beginning of the author's life and progresses chronologically to the day his/her manuscript goes off to the publisher. Your memoir will be a much more comfortable experience because that's the way you will plan it to be.

Activity:

The next time a pleasant moment from your past comes to mind, grab a notebook or a pad of paper and jot down a few words to describe it (but only a brief paragraph) on a page with nothing else on it. When you have finished, write the year that moment occurred, at the top of the page, then write nothing else on the same page again.

After you have a dozen pages like that (one page, one memory) you will be ready to continue to the "Fleshing out" phase, later.

Secret #4:

Your Memoirs can be just random memories if that's what you choose.

Beginning your memoir project might be easier for you if you don't think of it as "writing a book," at first. Think of it, instead, as only the collection of memories you have been jotting down as they occur to you.

Once you have collected, say, a dozen of those notes (each separate from the others) spread them all out on some "at surface (a bed, a kitchen table, a countertop, or even a floor) in any order. Imagine each chapter of your manuscript, which needs only to be expanded with more details on its subject. Each chapter may standalone to focus on just that memory (e.g., "Learning to read in the first grade"), or relate to others to complete a larger memory (e.g., "My elementary school years"). Because these are your memoirs (and not an autobiography), it is your choice whether to present these "chapters" chronologically, or as random as you please.

In the next tip, we'll talk about how to expand the "topic" memories you've compiled, one-to-a- page/card, into its own chapter by simply adding more details to each one. It will be time to think more about how you will want the finished product to look.

Activity:

Look at your notes on the flat surface before you and rearrange them several times: Randomly? Date-order? Combinations of both? This will have the dual benefit of giving you a clearer picture of how your manuscript will be organized, and it will generate new topics you want to add, either as more details or even new chapters from your past.

Secret #5:

"Flesh out" your Content - the FUN part

You have a dozen or more "topics," noted and dated, each on its own card or slip of paper. For the moment, let's think of them as "Chapters." Pick one at random, or whichever of them appeals to you most. From now on, whenever you have time to spend comfortably, select one topic and expand on its details, just noting anything else that comes to mind. Your topic card/page will soon become several more pages, and in later stages you will continue adding details, "fleshing out" each topic until it looks more like a complete chapter.

As before, adding the content is all that's important. Don't worry about spelling, grammar, and punctuation. It is more important that you use your conversational style of writing.

Also, don't worry about writing too many pages on any topic; more content is better than too little, because you can edit much of it out later.

Activity:

Begin fleshing out all your topics at your leisure, and as that process generates other memory topics, jot them down, too, for later fleshing out. This is an ongoing process that will continue even after you start the later stages of editing and publishing, if that's where you're going with this.

Secret #6:

DIY "Developmental Editing"

Even as you continue adding content and fleshing out topics to make chapters, you can begin the editing process, whether you farm out the work to a professional or do it yourself.

Developmental editing begins when you assemble the content you have created so far into coherent, connected, or semi-connected topics.

They need not be chronological, though that may be the simplest structure for many. I prefer what I call "quasichronological," which is beginning-to-end, but with "flashbacks" where you might interrupt one chapter with a related memory from the past.

. . .

You can also "flash forward" by noting a future result in a time you don't plan to be covering by itself later in your manuscript.

Remember, autobiographies cover all times, but your memoir will cover only those periods and events you decide you want to mention.

In your finished manuscript, a chapter may be only 3—5 pages long. Some may be much longer, but that is not your concern just yet.

Activity:

Continue fleshing out topics into chapter-length content, but don't form complete chapters yet. As this process continues, sort them into date-order. Once this developmental editing reaches the point that your manuscript looks like chapters in the book, you're only two steps from the finish: copyediting and proofreading.

SECRET #7:

To publish, or not to publish?

Don't let yourself be overwhelmed by this process; this summary of the steps is only an overview. The details of how to complete each step are covered more thoroughly in this book.

This might be a good time to go back to the beginning and review the goals you started with. And, yes, it is perfectly

O.K. to change those goals as you learn more about the process.

Even if you started out planning to publish your work for sale on Amazon, I would suggest that, until you have at least completed the developmental editing process, you write for your own pleasure first. There's plenty of time to tailor your work for public distribution as you proceed to the copy-editing stage.

Copyediting will be covered in more detail. It is essentially reviewing the printed pages, sentence-by-sentence and checking for things like continuity, spelling, punctuation, and syntax. It is the copy editor's job to be your "reader's advocate" and suggest changes to your manuscript that might make it more appealing to your audience.

. . .

A good copy editor might go through your entire text 10-12 times as you incorporate changes and additions. Considering a 100-page book is about 25,000 words, that's a lot of attention, but it's also a good reason to find a superb copy editor to do it right.

Once the copy editor is finished, he hands it over to a proofreader, who goes over it again with a final and even finer examination of things like capitalization, spelling, and punctuation before it goes out to the printer.

Activity:

Re-visit your goals often. Publish if you wish, but don't feel obliged to publish just because of all the time you put into your memoirs. Having done all that work, many and great satisfaction from re-discovering happy memories long forgotten or finding closure by finally putting unpleasant ones to rest.

At least one of my clients got unexpected relief from rereading her finished work in the peaceful comfort of her back porch, as it exposed traumas from her early childhood. She waived all royalties from the sale of the book because she got all the satisfaction she needed from the writing of it.

You can do that, too. Try it!

The Power of Sensory Details

There is a moment in almost every memoir I have edited when the writing suddenly comes alive. The author stops reporting events and starts inhabiting them. The shift is usually small—a single sentence that reaches beyond the facts and into the senses—and the effect on the reader is immediate and unmistakable. You stop reading about someone's life and start living it alongside them.

That shift is almost always the result of sensory details.

When Patsy wrote about the farmhouse where she grew up, she didn't just tell me it was old and crowded. She told me about the smell of kerosene from the lamp on the kitchen table, the way the floorboards in the hallway always announced your arrival no matter how carefully you stepped, and the scratchy weight of a wool blanket on a January night. Those details did something no list of facts could: they invited the reader inside.

You have that same power, and you may not even know it yet. The memories you carry are not stored in your brain as bullet points. They are stored as full sensory experiences—smells and textures and sounds—and when you learn to reach for those details as you write, your memoir will do something extraordinary. It will make the reader feel as though they were there.

The Five Doors into Memory

Think of each of the five senses as a door into a memory. Most first-time memoir writers reach for the most obvious door: sight. They describe what things looked like, who was standing where, and what the weather was like. That's a fine starting point, but the four other doors—sound, smell, touch, and taste—are often where the most powerful details are hiding.

Sound, for instance, has an almost magical ability to transport a reader. The hiss of a pressure cooker on a 1960s stovetop, the creak of a screen door in summer, the sound of your father's car pulling into the driveway at the end of a workday—any of those details can instantly conjure a world that would take three paragraphs of description to construct any other way.

Smell may be the most powerful memory trigger of all. Scientists have long noted that our sense of smell connects to the brain's memory and emotion centers more directly than any other sense. You have probably experienced this yourself: a particular perfume, a whiff of a certain food, the smell of rain on hot pavement, and suddenly you are ten years old again. When you can identify those trigger smells in your own memories and work them into your writing, readers will feel the same jolt of recognition.

Touch is often overlooked but enormously effective. The smooth wood of a much-handled tool, the cold weight of a coin pressed into your palm, the rough weave of a school uniform shirt—these physical sensations ground a scene in the body. They remind the reader that the person on the page was a real human being who occupied a real physical world.

Taste is perhaps the most personal of all the senses, and therefore the most intimate in memoirs. Food has a way of carrying entire worlds within it. A specific dish at a specific table can contain within it a whole family, a whole era, an entire set of relationships. If there are meals or tastes that stand out in your memories, take a moment to sit with them. What were you eating? Who made it? What did it mean to be at that table?

A Practical Exercise in Sensory Recall

Here is an exercise that many of my clients have found helpful. Choose a memory you have already noted on one of your index cards or pages—ideally one that takes place in a specific location: a kitchen, a schoolyard, a workplace, a car. Close your eyes and place yourself back in that scene.

Now work through the senses deliberately. What did it smell like? Not just—was there an odor—but what specifically? Was there something cooking? Something industrial or chemical? Cut grass? Cigarette smoke? Pine sap? Old paper? Spend a full minute just on smell before moving on.

Now sound. What were the ambient noises of that place? Not just voices, but background sounds—machinery, traffic, weather, music from another room, the collective hum of a cafeteria. Then touch: what surfaces did you encounter? What were you wearing, and how did it feel? Was the air warm or cold, humid or dry? And finally, was there anything you tasted in that memory, or nearby it in time?

Jot down whatever comes to mind. Don't edit. Even the smallest and most seemingly trivial detail is worth noting because you cannot know yet which detail will light up a reader the same way it lit up a corner of your memory.

A Word About Accuracy

You may wonder: what if I don't remember exactly? What if I'm uncertain whether the kitchen walls were yellow or cream, whether it was a Tuesday or a Wednesday, whether the song on the radio was the one I think it was?

This is a question every memoir writer faces, and it is worth addressing directly. You are not writing a court transcript. You are not filing an insurance claim. You are writing your memoir, which means you are writing about your experience of events as you remember them. Memory is not a recording; it is a reconstruction, and every person's reconstruction is their own. What you remember is true in the way that matters most: it is true to how those events lived in you.

If you are uncertain about a specific detail, you can signal that honestly in your text. "The walls were yellow, or maybe a pale green—I remember them as yellow." That kind of candor is not a weakness; it is one of the most endearing qualities a memoir can have. It reminds the reader that they are in the company of a real person, doing their best to hold on to something real.

The goal is not perfect accuracy. The goal is honest, vivid, felt experience. And sensory detail is how you get there.

Handling the Hard Stuff

Not every memory is pleasant, which is part of what makes a life a life. One of the most common questions I hear from people working on their memoirs is some version of this: Do I have to include the hard parts? If I do, how do I write about them without it feeling like I'm either making too much of them or glossing over them?

The short answer is no; you don't have to include anything you don't want to. Your memoir is yours. I think I said it plainly in the first pages of this book: one of the great freedoms of memoir versus autobiography is that you choose what goes in and what stays out. Nobody is grading you on completeness.

That said, many writers find that the hard memories—the ones they are most tempted to skip—are often the ones that matter most. Not because suffering is inherently meaningful, but because how a person moves through difficulty is one of the most revealing things about them. It is where character shows itself most clearly. And it is, very often, what readers find most recognizable about a life that is otherwise very different from their own.

Why hard things are often the most connecting

Here is a truth about reading memoirs: readers do not primarily connect with your best moments. They connect with your most human ones. The story of something going beautifully right is pleasant to read, but the story of something going badly wrong—and what you did next—is the one that stays with people.

This does not mean your memoir needs to be full of suffering. What it means is that you should not automatically protect yourself from including the moments that were complicated, painful, or embarrassing. Those moments, handled honestly, are often the most generous thing you can give a reader.

Think of it this way: somewhere out there, probably more than one person, is quietly living through something very similar to whatever hard thing you experienced. A difficult family relationship. A job loss. A health scare. A period of feeling lost. A decision they regret. When they encounter those experiences honestly rendered in a memoir —not dramatized, not minimized, just seen—they often feel, sometimes for the first time, that they are not alone in it. You will never know who those readers are. But they will know you.

Writing About Other People

The hardest part of including tough material is usually

not the events themselves, but the people involved in them. Most hard memories include at least one other person: someone who hurt you, someone you hurt, someone who let you down, or someone you let down. How do you write honestly about those experiences without turning your memoir into an act of score-settling?

First, a practical consideration: if you plan to publish your work, it is worth knowing that writing about real, living people carries some legal and ethical weight. You have wide latitude to write about your own experience of events, but attributing actions or motivations to specific named individuals, especially in ways that could damage their reputation, can create complications. When in doubt, consult a publishing professional or an attorney about what is safe.

Beyond the legal question, there is a craft question. The most effective memoir writing about difficult relationships focuses on behavior and experience rather than character judgments. Instead of telling the reader what kind of person someone was, show what they did and how it affected you. Let the reader draw their own conclusions. This approach is both more honest—because you genuinely cannot know what was in another person's heart—and more powerful, because the reader's own judgment, arrived at through the evidence you've provided, will carry far more weight than your verdict.

Many writers also find it helpful to change identifying details for supporting characters who play painful roles in their stories. A name, a location, a job title—minor adjustments can protect someone's privacy without distorting the emotional truth of the experience. If you change identifying details, it is good practice to note that you have done so in a brief author's note.

The Therapeutic Value of Writing Through Difficulties

I touched on something important in the story of Patsy: she found unexpected closure in the writing of her memoir. That experience is not unusual. There is something about putting a tough experience into ordered language—giving it a beginning, a middle, and an end, finding the words for it, getting it outside of yourself and onto a page—that many people find genuinely healing.

This does not mean memoir writing is a substitute for therapy, or that you should push yourself to write about things you are not ready to approach. If a particular memory feels too raw or too large to tackle right now, mark it on a card and set it aside. You may find that by the time you have built up some writing momentum with the easier material, the harder memories become more approachable.

But if you circle a particular memory—returning to it, thinking about it, feeling the pull of it without quite sitting down to write—that is often a sign that the memory has something to offer. Not necessarily to anyone who will ever read your memoir, but to you. Writing can be a way of finally looking directly at something you have been looking at sideways for years. And many people find that once they have done that, the memory loses some of its power over them.

A Practical Approach

If you are facing a hard memory and are not sure how to begin, try this: write it in the third person first. Instead of "I was twelve years old, and I didn't understand what was happening," write "A twelve-year-old girl stood in the kitchen and didn't understand what was happening." Distance, even artificial distance, can make a first draft easier to complete. Once the events are on the page in whatever form, you can go back and translate to the first person—or not. Some writers find the third-person distance serves memory better and choose to keep it.

Another approach is simply to write what happened, without yet writing how you felt about it. Facts first, feeling later. Get the sequence of events down—who, what, when, where—and return to the emotional layer in a second pass. This separation can keep the first draft from becoming overwhelming.

Whatever approach you use, remember that the first draft is for your eyes only. You are not publishing it, not showing it to anyone, not being judged on it. Write it as badly as you need to. Write it with all the anger, or grief, or confusion still in it. There will be time later to find the language that communicates rather than simply vents. But first, you need to get it out.

Telling Your Story Out Loud: The Recorded Memoir

Everything in this book so far has assumed that your memoir will be written. You will put words on paper—or on a screen—and those words will eventually form the document that tells your story. By far, the most common path. But it is not the only one.

Some people are natural storytellers in the spoken word who freeze the moment they are asked to write. Others are dealing with physical limitations that make writing difficult or impossible. Still others simply find that they tell their stories better when they are talking to someone—when there is a living human being on the other side of the exchange, asking follow-up questions, laughing at the right moments, keeping the story moving.

If any of that sounds like you, consider the recorded memoir.

What a Recorded Memoir Is

A recorded memoir is exactly what it sounds like: your stories captured in audio or video rather than in writing. It can take several forms. At its simplest, it is a series of recorded conversations in which you tell your stories out loud—to a family member, to a friend, or simply to a recording device set up in a quiet room. At its most elaborate, it can be a professionally produced oral history with multiple sessions, photography, and archival materials woven in.

For most people, the right approach is somewhere in the middle: a series of informal but purposeful conversations, recorded on a smartphone or a simple digital recorder, loosely organized around the same topics you might use as index cards for a written memoir. The result is an audio document that can be shared with family, stored in a digital archive, or—if you choose—transcribed and edited into a written manuscript.

That last point is worth emphasizing. A recorded memoir does not have to stay in audio form. Many people find it much easier to talk their memoir into existence first and then work with a transcription—either doing the editing themselves or hiring someone to help. The words that come out in a natural, relaxed conversation are often warmer and more alive than what the same person might produce sitting alone at a desk trying to write. Starting with speech and moving to text is a completely legitimate path to a written memoir.

Getting Started With Recording

The equipment barrier to a recorded memoir is lower than most people think. The smartphone in your pocket almost certainly has a voice memo or recording application that will produce perfectly usable audio. If you prefer something more purpose-built, a small digital voice recorder can be purchased for well under fifty dollars and will give you excellent quality for spoken words.

The more important preparation is not technical; it is structural. Before you sit down to record, spend a little time with the same index-card or note-taking process we recommended for a written memoir. Jot down the memories, events, and periods you want to cover. Group related ones together. Give yourself a rough map of the territory, even if you don't follow it precisely once you talk.

Then find your space. The same advice applies here as for written memoir: a quiet place where you feel comfortable and are unlikely to be interrupted. For recording, you'll also want to minimize background noise. A room with soft furnishings absorbs sound better than a bare kitchen or bathroom. Turn off televisions, fans, and other ambient noise sources. Close the windows if traffic is audible.

When you are ready, simply begin. You might start by stating the date and the memory or topic you plan to talk about. Then just talk. Tell the story the way you would tell it to a good friend over coffee. Don't worry about saying "um" or backing up to correct yourself or going on a tangent. A transcription can be edited. What matters in the first recording is that you get into the flow of telling.

The Interview Format

Many people find it much easier to tell their stories when someone else is asking questions. If that is true for you, the interview format may be your best path into a recorded memoir. Ask a family member, a close friend, or even an adult grandchild to sit with you for an hour or two and simply ask about your life.

Before the session, give your interviewer a list of topics or questions to draw from. You can take these directly from your index cards, or you can use a more general framework: early childhood memories, school years, work life, relationships, major decisions and turning points, things you learned, things you would do differently, things you are most proud of.

A good interviewer does not need to stick to the script. The best recorded memoir conversations follow their own logic—one story leads to another, a detail triggers a memory, an unexpected emotion surfaces and opens a door that wasn't on anyone's list. Encourage your interviewer to follow those threads, to ask, "What happened next?" and "How did that make you feel?" and "Do you remember what it looked like?" The sensory detail that we discussed in the previous chapter comes naturally in spoken conversation in a way that it sometimes doesn't in writing.

If no willing interviewer is available, there is another option that many people find surprisingly effective: record yourself answering written questions. Write out a list of questions—as many as you like, specific or broad—and then sit with the recorder running and read each question before answering it out loud. The act of responding to a question rather than a simple monologue is enough to shift many people into a more natural, story-telling mode.

Preserving and Sharing Recorded Memoirs

Once you have a set of recordings, the question of preservation becomes important. Audio and video files stored only on a single device are vulnerable: hard drives fail, phones are lost or broken. Make multiple copies and store them in multiple places. Cloud storage services provide one layer of protection; an external hard drive kept at a different location provides another. Family members who receive copies of the recordings are themselves archives.

For long-term preservation, audio files in standard formats—MP3, WAV, or FLAC—are your best bet. Most voice memo apps will allow you to export recordings in one of these formats. Video files in MP4 format are widely compatible and will be readable on the hardware and software of the foreseeable future.

If you plan to share your recorded memoir with family members, consider creating a simple document that accompanies the recordings: a list of the sessions with dates and topics, a few notes on who is speaking and who any named individuals are, and any historical or family context that might help a listener who wasn't there. Future generations who encounter these recordings may have very little context for who you were and when you lived; a brief guide can make your recordings far more meaningful to them.

From Recording to the Written Page

If you eventually want to move from a recorded memoir to a written one, transcription is your bridge. You can transcribe recordings yourself—time-consuming but deeply familiar—or you can use one of the several automated transcription services now available online, many of which are inexpensive and remarkably accurate for clearly spoken, noise-free audio. A human transcriptionist, hired through a freelancing platform, will give you the cleanest result if the audio quality is less than ideal.

A raw transcription of a spoken memoir will need editing before it reads well as a written document. Speech has rhythms and habits—repetition, self-correction, verbal filler—that serve us perfectly in conversation but look cluttered on the page. The editing process is not about changing what you said; it is about rendering it in the form most natural to a reader rather than a listener. Many people find this editing step easier than writing from scratch because the substance is already there. All you are doing is shaping it.

Whether you end up with a written memoir, a recorded one, or some combination of both, the most important thing is the same: you end up with something. A life lived and not recorded is a library burned. You have stories that no one else has. You have a perspective on events, on people, on decades that cannot be reconstructed from any other source. Whatever form you choose to capture it in, the act of capturing it is what matters.

So, begin. Not when you have the right notebook, or the

right chair, or the right amount of free time, or the right level of confidence. Begin today with whatever you have. A note on a scrap of paper. Thirty seconds of audio on your phone. One memory, written in whatever words come.

That is the beginning. Everything else follows.

Resources

The Resources pages are where the JMcontent* team shares some tools, reference books, websites, or articles we have found helpful in building our business and in running it every day. These pages are under continuous revision as we continue to grow, as resources change, and as new ones are added.

Any resources we include with which we don't have personal experience will, in each instance, be identified as such, but most are listed here because we and our experience with them has been outstanding.

Our recommendations are based on deep experience with and knowledge of these companies and their products. We recommend them because we have found them to be genuinely helpful.

Please spend no money on these products unless you believe they will help you achieve your goals.

*JMcontent, LLC is the parent company of the original blog (writethestoryofyou.com) from which this book is written.

Tools

PerfectIt: http://www.intelligentediting.com

PerfectIt is a tool for editors and proofreaders to check any content for spelling, punctuation, capitalization, and consistency.

We like it because you can change it to do its many tasks tailored to the specific needs of a single person, project, or company's style preferences, and it is one of the most inexpensive annual subscriptions of any tool we use.

For example, let's say you have written ten pages of a document or manuscript (your memoir? A case study for your boss?) and you check it for consistency using PerfectIt.

One or two clicks at the top of your MS Word page lets you run the program through its paces. You simply make choices as it asks for your preferences for consistent use of a term, spelling of a word or an abbreviation, certain punctuation marks, and so on, one-at-a-time.

(Want to see a two-minute video demo? Check this link): http://www.intelligentediting.com

GoDaddy: *https://www.godaddy.com/*

GoDaddy is the service we have used to host our sites online for the past ten years. We switched to them when we were about to lose all our online content because our previous hosting company wouldn't communicate with the one that registered our domains.

GoDaddy's superb support team switched both the domain and the hosting to its service, and we haven't had a problem since. Of other popular hosting services online, some are less expensive than GoDaddy, but we feel sincerely that the superior support it offers is more than enough to justify any price difference.

Reference Books

"The Blue Book of Grammar and Punctuation," *by Jane Straus*

This is an easy-to-use reference guide and workbook we keep, not on our bookshelf, but on our desk, within easy reach. It is a 100-page paperback good for quick-reference, and well-organized for rapid responses to questions on major grammar and punctuation issues.

We usually get ours on eBay for a few dollars. They are used, but we rarely find a mark on them, and they serve us well.

"GRAMMAR RULES," *by Craig Shrives*

The subtitle of this 250-page hardback book is, "Writing with Military Precision," and its author is a military man who put it together after learning to appreciate the critical need for clear communication in battlefield conditions.

The volume is a little bigger than pocketbook size, but small enough to fit easily in an average briefcase. For its small size, though, it is remarkably thorough as a refresher of the rules you forgot or ignored in high school.

It has been in print since 2011, but like so many of our references, we usually get them (used) from eBay for a few well-invested dollars.

Websites

Comma Sense: Your Guide to Grammar Victory
Available in print and digital editions, this is the one grammar book you'll want to keep at your fingertips, no matter what kind of writing and editing you do.

GRAMMAR MONSTER: *https://www.grammar-monster.com/*
This is a great (FREE) site that reinforces what you know about grammar and punctuation and coaches you on where you might need some improvement. It can be useful for all levels, from newcomers to the language to professors of the subject.

Draft 2 Digital: https://draft2digital.com/ Draft 2 Digital (D2D) recently merged with my favorite self-publishing house, "Smashwords," and the "Best-in-the-Business" got instantly better (in my opinion). I was publishing my last book when my formatter told me about D2D, and working with the new team was a gift from the gods!

FORMATTING: I'm also happy to recommend that formatter most highly. When you need one, from my experience, you can't do better. She is: [**Brooke Gilbert**], and here's how you can reach her: [www.brookegilbertauthor.etsy.com or brookegilbertauthor@gmail.com.

Free Help With Your Writing Skills!

If doubting your skill as an author is holding you back, here's a **free** course in writing from Henneke, my favorite blogger on the subject:

https://www.enchantingmarketing.com/free-writing-course/

Henneke is one of my most favorite writers, and her periodic posts and newsletters are always a fun read, and a great source of ideas on how better to express yourself. Once you receive her notes, you'll look forward to them like an old chum dropping in for a friendly visit.

About the Author

We hope you enjoyed this book and that it might encourage you to think about writing your own memoir. All links and other details were current at the time of publishing in 2026.

If you found this book to be helpful, please leave an honest review of your experience with the content on Amazon or Goodreads.

Most of all, we wish you the pleasure you will discover in telling the **Story of YOU!**

www.ingramcontent.com/pod-product-compliance
Lightning Source LLC
LaVergne TN
LVHW090617110826
845146LV00001B/427

* 9 7 9 8 9 9 0 1 3 5 6 0 4 *